DID YOU KNOW?

Saudi Arabia is the largest country in the world without a river.

Aogashima is an isolated village in Tokyo that resides INSIDE a volcano with another mini volcano inside it.

In Russia, women outnumber men by 10 million.

The small strings inside bananas are phloem bundles and have the important job of distributing nutrients throughout the fruit.

Mosquitoes have two eyes, each consisting of hundreds of lenses which enable them to see from many directions and angles at once.

North Korean President Kim Jong-un travels with his own toilet to prevent others from being able to analyze his waste excretions to determine his health status.

DID YOU KNOW?

The oldest hotel in the world has been operated by the same Japanese family for over 1300 years. More than 52 different generations of descendants have operated the inn.

———•———

Kangaroo rats never drink water during their entire lifetime.

———•———

The longest tunnel in the world is 57km long and is located between Switzerland to Italy underneath The Alps. It took 17 years to construct.

———•———

A baby in the mother's womb sends cells to fix any damage in a pregnant woman.

———•———

A blue whale's heart can weigh as much as a car.

———•———

Doctors used to use spiderwebs to make bandages.

DID YOU KNOW?

Geese have ridges on their tongues for straining aquatic plants in the water.

———·———

Brazil is the world's largest coffee producing country.

———·———

Penguins are the only bird who can swim underwater but cannot fly.

———·———

Elephants sleep for only 2 hours per day.

———·———

You can't burp in space.

———·———

The longest street in the world is Yonge Street in Toronto, Canada at 1178 miles long.

———·———

Baby elephants are born blind.

———·———

The only bird who can fly backward is the hummingbird.

DID YOU KNOW?

"Chocolate cosmos" is a flower which smells like chocolate.

The National Animal of Scotland is the unicorn.

Wat Pa Maha Chedi Kaew is a Buddhist temple in Thailand which is constructed of 1.5 million beer bottles.

There is an abandoned city in Turkey called Burj Al Babas which contains over 500 empty castles.

King Cobra is the only species of snake to build nests.

Vulture bees substitute meat for pollen and still make honey from nectar.

Penguins mate, nest & raise their chicks in a rookery.

DID YOU KNOW?

Ostrich eyes are the size of billiard balls.

A group of porcupines is called a prickle.

Pumice stone is hardened volcanic lava and contains so many air bubbles that it is light enough to float in water.

The human body contains about 37.2 trillion cells.

The average human heart beats around 100,000 times a day.

The Amazon rainforest is the largest tropical rainforest in the world covering 5.5 million square kilometers.

Human bones are 5x stronger than steel of the same density.

DID YOU KNOW?

Native Australian lyrebird is known for being a master of mimicry, copying sounds like chainsaws and camera clicks, which the males use to attract mates.

The nocturnal bird Frogmouth is an expert in camouflage, blending into tree bark and making it one of nature's most stealth predators.

The Vogelkop Superb Bird-of-Paradise has a courtship dance where it turns itself into a black oval shape with a vivid blue face and it looks like a floating smiley face.

The horned lizard can squirt blood from it's eyes as a defense mechanism.

Male lions with darker manes are considered more attractive to females.

New York City features over 800 spoken languages.

DID YOU KNOW?

The tallest tree species in the world is the coast redwood (Sequoia sempervirens).

The world's largest salt flat is Salar de Uyuni, Bolivia.

Paris' nickname the "City of Light" began when it was the first city to install streetlights.

Cairo is known as the "City of a Thousand Minarets" because of it's numerous mosques.

There are more hydrogen atoms in a single molecule of water than there are stars in the entire solar system.

When male & female anglerfish mate, they melt into each other and share bodies forever. Once he latches on and fuses to her, he loses his eyes & internal organs until they share a bloodstream.

DID YOU KNOW?

The tallest tree species in the world is the coast redwood (Sequoia sempervirens).

---·---

The world's largest salt flat is Salar de Uyuni, Bolivia.

---·---

Paris' nickname the "City of Light" began when it was the first city to install streetlights.

---·---

Cairo is known as the "City of a Thousand Minarets" because of it's numerous mosques.

---·---

There are no words in the English language that rhyme with "month" or "orange".

---·---

When male & female anglerfish mate, they melt into each other and share bodies forever. Once he latches on and fuses to her, he loses his eyes & internal organs until they share a bloodstream.

DID YOU KNOW?

It would take 19 minutes to fall to the center of the Earth.

The real name for a hashtag is an octothorpe.

The longest English word is 189,819 letters long.

The tiny pocket in jeans was designed to store pocket watches.

People once ate arsenic to improve their skin.

The largest bowling alley in the world is located in Japan and features 116 bowling lanes.

The Terminator script was sold for $1.

DID YOU KNOW?

The moon looks upside down in the Southern Hemisphere.

You can be pregnant and not realize it. Cryptic pregnancies are not uncommon and 1 in 500 is not recognized until halfway through pregnancy, while 1 in 2500 is not known until labor begins.

Starfish don't technically have bodies. Their entire bodies are classified as heads.

There are more bacterial cells in your body than human cells, however since human cells weigh more, 99.7% of the body is human cells.

Most orange cats are males. Orange cats are typically 3:1 males over females.

Your nails grow faster in hot temperatures which is why you need to trim your nails more often during summertime.

DID YOU KNOW?

Platypuses sweat milk because it doesn't have teats. Milk appears as sweat would, but it's an aquatic animal so it doesn't sweat at all.

An ordinary LEGO plastic brick is able to support the weight of 375,000 other bricks before it fails which means it withstands compression better than concrete.

A rainbow on Venus is called a glory.

Mirrors facing each other don't produce infinite reflections. Each reflection will be darker than the last, eventually fading into invisibility.

All mammals get goosebumps.

The largest butterfly in the world has a 31 cm wingspan.

DID YOU KNOW?

Lightning bolts are 5x hotter than the sun's surface temperature.

On average, a human can hold their breath between 30-90 seconds underwater.

Dogs tilt their heads when spoken to in order to help them pinpoint where the noise is coming from more quickly.

Flamingoes aren't born pink, they are actually born with grey & white feathers and develop the pinkish hue after beginning a diet of brine shrimp & blue-green algae.

Many species of ants give off scents. Trap-jaw ants release a chocolate smell when annoyed and citronella ants give off a lemony scent.

Beavers don't live in dams. They live in lodges they construct behind the dam, within a deep pool of water.

DID YOU KNOW?

It rains liquid methane on Saturn's largest moon.

When Apollo 16 astronaut Charles Duke landed on the Moon in 1972 he left a family photo behind, which remains there to this day.

Giraffes hum to communicate with one another.

People have a 50% chance of sharing a birthday with a friend. In a random group of 23 people, two people will share a birthday.

"New car smell" is actually a mix of over 200 chemicals.

Pine trees can predict rain. If the air is humid pinecones will close, anticipating upcoming rain.

DID YOU KNOW?

Your brain burns 400-500 calories per day.

Rhythm is the longest English word without a vowel.

Porcupines float in water.

Peaches are related to almonds.

Hawaii is the only state with one school district.

The original recipe for chocolate contained chili powder instead of sugar.

In ancient Rome, lemons were used as a poison antidote.

A chef's hat has 100 folds. In the early days, the number of pleats in a chef's hat indicated how many recipes or techniques they had mastered.

DID YOU KNOW?

The Anglo-Zanzibar War was the shortest in history, lasted only 38 minutes in 1896 between Britain & Zanzibar.

Bananas are classified as berries.

Octopus have three hearts which help them survive in the ocean depths where oxygen levels are low.

The world's largest snowflake was recorded in 1887 in Montana and measured 15" wide and 8" thick.

The wood frog can freeze solid during winter then thaw out and hop away when the weather warms up due to special proteins in their body which prevent damage.

Sea cucumbers can eject their guts as a defense mechanism to scare off predators.

DID YOU KNOW?

The mudskipper fish can walk on land using pectoral fins like legs, and can even climb trees.

Blue whales consume up to half a million calories in a single mouthful of krill.

Sloths can hold their breath up to 40 minutes, longer than most dolphins.

Underneath their thick white fur, polar bears actually have black skin which helps them absorb and retain heat from the sun.

The shortest commercial flight in the world lasts only 57 seconds between the islands of Westray & Papa Westray in Scotland, covering just 1.7 miles.

Avocados are a fruit not a vegetable.

The heart of a shrimp is located in it's head.

DID YOU KNOW?

Ancient Romans used to drop a piece of toast into their wine for good health, which is where we get "raise a toast" from.

It's illegal to own a single guinea pig in Switzerland as it's considered animal abuse since they are social beings.

When we take a warm shower, we experience increased dopamine flow which makes us more creative.

The only letter that doesn't appear in any American state name is Q.

Queen Elizabeth II was a trained mechanic from the age of 16 when she joined the British Labour Exchange and learned the basics of truck repair.

DID YOU KNOW?

M&Ms are named after the businessmen who created them: Forrest Mars & Bruce Murrie. Mars leveraged Murrie out of his 20% share of the business before it became big.

The actors who voiced Mickey & Minnie Mouse married in real life in 1991 (Russi Taylor - Minnie & Wayne Allwine - Mickey)

The last letter added to the English alphabet was "J" back in 1524.

Ketchup was once sold as medicine for those with indigestion back in 1834.

The world's longest walking distance is 14K miles from Magadan in Russian to Cape Town in South Africa with no flying or sailing, just bridges and roads.

Humans are the only animals that blush.

DID YOU KNOW?

An ostrich's eye is bigger than it's brain.

A jiffy is an actual unit of time, it's 1/100th of a second.

You can't hum if you hold your nose.

Vatican City is the smallest country in the world, 120x smaller than the island of Manhattan.

A crocodile cannot stick it's tongue out.

Pigs can't look up into the sky.

In the course of an average lifespan, you could eat 70 different insects and 10 spiders while sleeping.

Everyone's tongue print is different, just like your fingerprint.

DID YOU KNOW?

People used to say "prunes" instead of "cheese" when getting photos taken. In the 1840s a London photographer had them say it to keep their mouths tight.

———•———

The blob of toothpaste on a toothbrush has a name, called a "nurdle".

———•———

The most popular letter in the alphabet is E.

———•———

Candles were once made from beef fat or bees wax so were typically stolen and eaten during times of famine.

———•———

KFC is the meal of choice on Christmas Day in Japan, thanks to a successful marketing campaign over 40 years ago.

———•———

Bamboo is the fastest growing woody plant in the world, growing up to 35" per day.

DID YOU KNOW?

Only 10% of the population is left-handed and men are more likely than women.

Cats spend an average of 15 hours a day sleeping.

With a global population of around 8 billion, you statistically share your birthday with around 19 million people worldwide.

There are about 5000 species of sea sponges.

The Pope cannot be an organ donor. All popes' bodies belong to the Vatican when they die, which means no organ donation is allowed.

The continent of Africa spans all four hemispheres.

After water, tea is the most consumed drink around the world.

DID YOU KNOW?

During the 2024 Summer Olympics, four sports made a debut: climbing, breaking, skateboarding & surfing.

Nepal has the most public holidays with 39 each year.

Sheffield FC is the oldest football club recognized by FIFA, founded in 1857.

The hottest temperature recorded on Earth was 134 degrees F taken in Death Valley, Nevada in July 1913.

If you Google the word "askew" the entire page will tilt.

The name LEGO came from the Danish words "Leg Godt" which means "play well".

Muhammed is the most popular name in the world.

DID YOU KNOW?

The tongue has about 8000 taste buds and the average person produces enough spit to fill about 500 bathtubs in their lifetime.

Pigeons have been trained to help the U.S. Coast Guard find people lost at sea.

Before mercury, brandy was used to fill thermometers.

The first telephone book only had 50 names in 1878.

There are more castles in Germany than McDonalds in the United States.

Caves in Missouri store 1.4 billion pounds of government-owned cheese.

Canadians eat 55% more Kraft Mac & Cheese than Americans.

DID YOU KNOW?

A grizzly bear's bite is strong enough to crush a bowling ball.

Woodpeckers wrap their tongue around their brains to help protect it from injury while pecking.

Pound cake got it's name from the original recipe which used one pound of each ingredient.

In the Great Barrier Reef there is a coral reef taller than the Empire State Building.

On average, lightning strikes Earth 100 times per second.

Due to genes, redheads may need 20% more anesthesia than non-redheads.

Barbie's full name is Barbara Millicent Roberts.

DID YOU KNOW?

There is a church in Czechia decorated with the bones of 40,000 people.

There are more fake flamingos in the world than real ones.

Up to one-third of a living bone's weight is water.

The closest U.S. state to Africa is Maine.

Armadillos almost always give birth to identical quadruplets.

Frogs actually use their eyes to help swallow meals. When it swallows food, it's eyes pull down to the roof of their mouth to help push food down it's throat.

Tigers skin is identical to their fur with striped markings like tattoos.

DID YOU KNOW?

From the sky deck of the Willis Tower in Chicago on a clear day you can see four other U.S. states: Illinois, Michigan, Indiana & Wisconsin.

A French general gave John Quincy Adams an alligator as a gift which was kept in one of the White House's bathtubs.

From 1924-1954 stop signs were yellow, until sign makers began using fade-resistant enamel and red was able to be used successfully.

Abraham Lincoln is honored in the Wrestling Hall of Fame and was inducted in 1992 as an "Outstanding American". He often competed in wrestling matches in his youth and rarely lost.

Among the world's five oceans, the Atlantic Ocean is the saltiest.

DID YOU KNOW?

A polar bear's fur isn't white, it's translucent. It appears white because of light reflection.

The fastest-moving muscle in the human body is the eyes.

Beer was banned in Iceland until 1989.

California experiences over 100,000 earthquakes each year, but most are minor or barely felt.

A housefly's feet are 10 million times more sensitive than a human tongue.

Owls sometimes swallow their food whole.

About 10,000 cells in your body could fit on the head of a pin.

The Empire State Building has it's own zip code - 10118.

DID YOU KNOW?

The original 3 Musketeers bars came in 3pks with a different nougat in each: vanilla, chocolate or strawberry. WW2 rations made it too expensive so it was cut to one.

Sudan has 255 pyramids which is more than any other country in the world, including Egypt which has 138 discovered.

If a child's entire circulatory system (veins, arteries, capillaries) were laid out flat, it would stretch more than 60,000 miles. Adults stretch more than 100,000 miles.

German chocolate cake is not named after the country in Europe, but after Sam German who created a mild dark baking chocolate bar for Baker's Chocolate Company in 1852.

DID YOU KNOW?

The Philippines is an archipelago (a group of islands) that number 7,641, which doesn't include thousands of sandbars which emerge during low tide.

The Trans-Siberian Railway is the longest railroad in Russia & the world. The journey takes seven days, during which passengers pass through eight different time zones and cross 3901 bridges.

There is enough gold in Earth's core to coat the entire surface of the Earth in 1.5 feet of gold.

The name of the food Spam is a combo of "spice" and "ham".

It would take a drop of water 90 days to travel the entire length of the Mississippi River which is 2340 miles long.

DID YOU KNOW?

The only muscle that never tires is the heart.

If you walked 12 hours a day, it would take the average person 690 days to walk around the world.

You are 1 cm taller in the morning than at night due to soft cartilage between your bones getting compressed.

The entire surface of your skin is replaced every month.

The average human body has 2.5 million sweat pores.

Every minute you shed over 30,000 dead skin cells.

All British armored vehicles have the equipment needed to make tea.

DID YOU KNOW?

The opposite sides of a die (one pair of dice) will always equal 7.

No number before 1000 contains the letter "A" when spelled out.

There are 293 ways to make change for a dollar.

Play-Doh was originally used as wallpaper cleaner.

You can get cell phone service on the top of Mount Everest.

The five-cent coin called nickel is actually only made of 25% nickel and the other 75% is copper.

Movie trailers originally played after the movie finished.

There are 31,557,600 seconds in a year.

DID YOU KNOW?

You cannot sneeze with your eyes open.

Farts are fast and travel almost 7 mph.
Coughs can travel at 60 mph and sneezes at
100 mph.

The acid in your stomach can dissolve steel.

The human nose can detect a trillion different
scents.

Human noses and ears never stop growing.

Women's hearts beat faster than men's.

Humans lose 50-100 hairs per day.

Boys have fewer taste buds than girls.

You cannot smell while you sleep.

Brown is the most common eye color.

DID YOU KNOW?

The body's largest organ is skin.

It takes your body 12 hours to fully digest food.

Your nose gets warmer when you tell a lie.

About half of the bones in your body are in your hands and feet.

Your arm span is about equal to your height.

When cranberries are ripe, they can bounce like a ball.

Apples are part of the rose family.

A jar of Nutella is sold every 2.5 seconds.

There is no butter in peanut butter.

You can still see traces of Neil Armstrong's footprints on the moon.

DID YOU KNOW?

The U.S. Treasury printed $100,000 bills between 1934 and 1935 which were never released to the public.

Before becoming president, Abraham Lincoln lost 5 different elections.

The earliest hockey pucks were made out of frozen cow poop.

Former NBA basketball star Shaquille O'Neal wears a size 23 shoe. The average male shoe size is 10.5.

The first golf balls were stuffed with bird feathers.

Tug-of-war used to be an Olympic sport.

In the early days of baseball, umpires sat in rocking chairs behind home plate.

DID YOU KNOW?

According to the United Nations, there are 195 recognized countries in the world.

Alaska is both the westernmost and easternmost state in the United States.

Greenland is the world's largest island.

Antarctica is the only continent with no permanent human residents.

Dust from the Sahara Desert in Africa can travel as far as Texas.

The state of California has more people than the entire country of Canada.

The Dead Sea is the lowest place on the planet.

Russia is just two miles from Alaska.

The world's largest desert is Antarctica.

DID YOU KNOW?

Mosquitoes are twice as attracted to the color blue than any other color.

Most toilet paper sold for residential use in France is pink.

The Boston Marathon didn't allow female runners until 1972.

A dime has 118 ridges around the edge.

Dragonflies lifespan is 24 hours.

Goldfish have a memory span of 3 seconds.

Al Capone's business card identified him as a used furniture dealer.

All 50 states are listed across the top of the Lincoln Memorial on the back of the $5 bill.

Babies are born without kneecaps and kids don't develop them until ages 2-6.

DID YOU KNOW?

Cats have over 100 vocal sounds, but dogs have only 10.

February 1865 is the only month in recorded history without a full moon.

The average American will spend a total of 6 months over a lifetime waiting at red traffic lights.

Leonardo Da Vinci invented the scissors.

Maine is the only state whose name is one syllable.

On a Canadian two dollar bill, the flag flying over the Parliament building is an American flag.

Peanuts are an ingredient in dynamite.

Rubber bands last longer when refrigerated.

DID YOU KNOW?

The average person's hand does 56% of the typing.

The cruiseliner QE2 moves six inches for every gallon of diesel it burns.

The microwave was invented after a researcher walked by a radar tube and a chocolate bar melted in his pocket.

The words "racecar", "kayak" and "level" are palindromes.

There is no Betty Rubble in the Flintstones Chewables Vitamins.

Typewriter is the longest word that can be made using the letters on only one row of the keyboard.

Fish never sleep.

DID YOU KNOW?

99% of all mazes can be solved if you walk to the right every time you have to choose between right and left.

Intelligent people have more zinc and copper in their hair.

The can opener was invented 48 years after cans were introduced.

When you lick a stamp you consume 1/10 of a calorie.

A silverback gorilla could deadlift 1800 lbs.

In Singapore when you turn 21 you are automatically registered as an organ donor.

The Apollo missions have left 96 bags of poo, pee & vomit on the moon.

DID YOU KNOW?

More than $700 million worth of aluminum cans are thrown out by Americans each year.

Roosters have built-in earplugs so they don't go deaf from crowing.

Elephants can swim for up to six hours at a time.

The only letters which don't appear on the periodic table are J and Q.

If a polar bear & grizzly bear mate, their offspring is called a "pizzy bear".

The ten highest mountain summits in the U.S. are all located in Alaska.

Daniel Radcliffe was allergic to his *Harry Potter* glasses (nickel allergy).

DID YOU KNOW?

Hershey's Kisses are named after the kissing sound the chocolate makes as it falls from the machine onto the conveyor belt.

If you cut down a saguaro cactus in Arizona, you can be charged with a class 4 felony & penalized with jail time.

The flashes of colored light you see when you rub your eyes are called "phosphenes".

At birth, a baby panda is smaller than a mouse.

Iceland does not have a railway system.

The world's largest grand piano was built by a 15 year old in New Zealand and measures over 18 feet long with 85 keys (3 short of the standard 88).

There are more LEGO minifigures than people on Earth.

DID YOU KNOW?

Approximately 50% of all gold ever mined on Earth came from Witwatersrand in South Africa.

75% of the world's diet is produced from 12 plants and five different animal species.

IKEA is an acronym that stands for Ingvar Kamprad Elmtaryd Agunnaryd (the founder's name, farm where he grew up & hometown).

Even standing around burns calories. A 150 lb person burns 114 calories per hour while standing and doing nothing.

GPS is free for the world to use, but it costs $2 million per day to operate, which comes from American tax revenue.

The color red doesn't really make bulls angry since they are color blind.

DID YOU KNOW?

Lettuce is a member of the sunflower family.

A cluster of bananas is called a "hand" and a single banana is called a "finger".

A wildlife technician, Richard Thomas, took the famous tongue twister "How much wood would a woodchuck chuck if a woodchuck could chuck wood" and calculated a rough estimate of 700 pounds.

If you heat up a magnet it will lose it's magnetism.

More tornadoes occur in the United Kingdom per square mile than in any other country in the world.

Times Square was originally called Longacre Square until it was renamed in 1904 after The New York Times moved it's HQ to the newly built Times Building.

DID YOU KNOW?

One of the World Trade Centers was built to be 1776 feet tall purposefully to reference the year the Declaration of Independence was signed.

———•———

"Tsundoku" is a Japanese word for the habit of purchasing too many books and letting them pile up without reading them.

———•———

Even though Irish is the official language of Ireland, Polish is more widely spoken.

———•———

In Japan, Domino's began testing pizza delivery via reindeer in 2016.

———•———

Helen Keller was related to Robert E. Lee, her paternal grandmother was second cousins with him.

———•———

Starfish don't have blood, instead they circulate nutrients by using seawater in their vascular system.

DID YOU KNOW?

Mount Rushmore cost less than $1 million to construct and took 400 workers 14 years.

On average, 46% of Americans have less than $10,000 in assets when they die.

While shedding, geckos will eat their skin in order to prevent predators from finding and eating them easily.

Bees have knees. The expression "bees knees" comes from how they store large build-ups of pollen in hairy baskets on their knees.

During the entire run of *Gilligan's Island*, it was never revealed if "Gilligan" was his first or last name.

Mona Lisa was stolen from the Louvre in 1911, which drew more visitors to see the empty space than the actual painting.

DID YOU KNOW?

Volvo invented the three-point seatbelt, then gave the invention away for free as they decided it's importance was too large to keep themselves.

———— • ————

The thumbs up sign is believed to have begun with Chinese pilots as a communication with the ground crew before takeoff.

———— • ————

The British Pound is the world's oldest currency still in use at 1200 years old.

———— • ————

The Great Pyramid of Giza actually has eight sides instead of four like all the other pyramids.

———— • ————

When we're born, the only innate fears we have are the fear of falling & and the fear of loud sounds. All other fears are learned.

———— • ————

The Eiffel Tower is repainted every seven years without closing to the public.

DID YOU KNOW?

Before finally being accepted, J.K. Rowling's original "Harry Potter" pitch was rejected by 12 publishers.

Garlic is known to attract leeches.

In 1992 a shipping crate containing 28,000 rubber duckies fell overboard and continued washing up around the world for the next 20 years.

A 26-sided shape is known as a rhombicuboctahedron.

There are over 6000 known species of grass.

The total weight of all air on Earth is 11 quintillion pounds.

Ant queens can live for up to 30 years.

DID YOU KNOW?

In 1962 the London Bridge (constructed in 1831) was sold to Lake Havasu City, Arizona to help tourism.

Captive tigers in the U.S. alone outnumber the amount of wild tigers worldwide.

1/3 of cats don't seem affected by catnip.

Barry Manilow wrote many famous jingles for companies like McDonald's, State Farm & BandAids.

Zebras have only one toe on each foot.

Over 9000 Blockbuster stores existed at it's peak, now only one store remains in Bend, Oregon.

There is a geocache on the ISS placed in 2008 and it has since been visited four times by other astronauts.

DID YOU KNOW?

In 1866 the U.S. purchased Alaska from Russia for $7.2 million paid via check.

When puppies are born they are completely blind and deaf, the first sense they develop is the sense of touch.

Any prime number higher than three, when squared and subtracted by one, will always turn out to be a multiple of 24.

The hand and footprints in front of the Chinese Theater tradition started accidently when silent film actress Norma Talmadge stepped on wet cement.

Snakes can help predict earthquakes from 75 miles away and up to five days before it happens.

Approximately 1 in every 2000 babies are born with a tooth.

DID YOU KNOW?

The Young America Township in Minnesota has a population of less than 1000 people but more than 20 zip codes.

Nutella was invented during WW2 when an Italian pastry maker mixed hazelnuts into chocolate to extend his chocolate ration.

Michael Jackson's shiny glove was just a modified golf glove.

Mr. & Mrs. originated from using the words master and mistress.

1912 was the last time Olympic medals were made entirely out of gold.

The little piece of paper sticking out of a Hershey's Kiss is called a niggly wiggly.

Eating grapefruit can interfere with 43 different kinds of medications.

DID YOU KNOW?

When cellophane was invented in 1908 it was originally intended to be used to protect tablecloths from wine spills.

In the 1980s, Fredric Baur (founder of Pringles) requested to be buried in a Pringles can and his children honored it.

The only window that opens on the presidential car is the driver's window to pay tolls. It has no keyholes and only the Secret Service knows how to open the doors.

Thomas Edison invented an electric pen in 1876 that was later adapted to become the first tattoo machine in 1891.

The sound of a Star Wars lightsaber was created by pairing together the sound of an idle film projector & the buzz from an old TV.

DID YOU KNOW?

Movie theaters make 85% of their profit off concession stands since ticket revenues have to be shared with movie distributors.

Mixing nonoplatelets from root vegetables like carrots along with cement can significantly strengthen it.

People who donate blood in Sweden are sent a text message every time their blood saves a life.

The average U.S. household has accumulated 30,000 "things", from paper clips to cars.

American children make up 3.7% of children on the planet but have 47% of all toys and children's books.

Motel 6 & Super 8 got their names from the original prices of rooms. Motel 6 began at $6 in 1962 and Super 8 at $8.88 in 1974.

DID YOU KNOW?

The German Autobahn has no speed limits.

Researchers have found that the smaller the testicles, the louder the monkey.

When double rainbows occur, the colors of the second arc are always reversed.

Kraft Singles cannot be advertised as cheese because the USDA standards state a food can only be identified as cheese if it contains "at least 51% real cheese".

It costs nearly $290,000 per year in fees to run a hot dog cart near the Central Park Zoo in New York City, which doesn't include cart incurred costs.

All of the sweaters that Mister Rogers wore on his show were handknitted by his mother.

Herring fish communicate by using flatulence.

DID YOU KNOW?

27,000 trees are cut down every day to supply the world's toilet paper.

Only 2% of the world's population has green eyes.

The first band to ever perform live on all seven continents was *Metallica*.

Spacesuits take 5000 hours to make, cost $1 million, weigh 110 pounds and have 11 layers of material.

The least common day to be born is May 22.

85% of Valentine's Day cards are bought by women.

Gatorade was invented to help the Florida Gators football team stay hydrated.

DID YOU KNOW?

It takes 7-8 trees to provide enough oxygen for one person for one year.

Arizona driver's licenses don't expire until you're 65, then you have to renew every five years in person.

Every day in the U.S. more than 100,000 people get a speeding ticket.

The largest purchaser of explosives in the United States is the U.S. Department of Defense. The second largest purchaser is Disney World.

Mountain Dew is slang for moonshine. It was originally created as a mixer for moonshine and whiskey in Tennessee.

About 70% of people tilt their heads to the right when kissing someone.

DID YOU KNOW?

If your throat tickles, you can scratch your ear to make it go away.

———————•———————

Even though smoking is banned on airplanes, ashtrays are mandatory for safe disposal in case someone breaks the law.

———————•———————

79% of pet owners sleep with their pets.

———————•———————

Brussels Airport is the world's biggest chocolate seller, selling over 800 tons of chocolate per year.

———————•———————

Harry Burnett Reese (founder of Reese's chocolate) was a former shipping foreman and dairy farmer for Milton S. Hershey, the founder of Hershey's chocolate.

———————•———————

Carrots have zero fat content.

———————•———————

The Cesky Terrier is the rarest breed of dog in the world, only 350 exist worldwide.

DID YOU KNOW?

When he was President, George H.W. Bush banned broccoli from Air Force One and The White House.

White chocolate doesn't have chocolate in it. It's simply a mixture of sugar, milk, vanilla, lecithin & cocoa butter.

Farmed salmon are fed specific plant pigments to give them a pink hue to match that of wild salmon.

Red Skittles are dyed with carminic acid, made from the crushed bodies of a beetle called the Dactylopius Coccus. It's used in maraschino cherries, strawberry & raspberry candy & lipstick.

It took until 2013 for Russia to classify beer as alcohol. Before that beer and other alcohol under 10% ABV was classified as a soft drink.

DID YOU KNOW?

McDonald's sells 2.5 billion hamburgers each year.

How many licks does it take to get to the center of a Tootsie Pop? In a study it ranged from 144 to 411 with the average 364 licks.

Eating pufferfish is a delicacy in Japan, but chefs have to train for over two years in order to qualify to serve it. If prepared incorrectly, it can kill the person eating it.

French fries originated in Belgium, not France.

Twinkie cream isn't really cream, it's vegetable shortening.

Potatoes are 80% water.

Pule cheese is made from donkey milk in Serbia and costs over $1000 per pound.

DID YOU KNOW?

In America, the go-to movie snack is popcorn, but it varies by country. In Columbia it's dried ants. In Korea, it's dried cuttlefish and in China it's dried salted plums.

———————•———————

The only difference between brown sugar & white sugar is that some of the molasses removed in the refining process is added back in to brown sugar.

———————•———————

The difference between jam and jelly is that jam is made from fruit (why it contains chunks) and jelly is made from fruit juice.

———————•———————

India has the lowest meat consumption in the world. Per capita, Indians only consume 7 pounds of meat per person per year.

———————•———————

Fortune cookies are not Chinese. They were invented in the early 1900s in San Francisco.

DID YOU KNOW?

Goat meat accounts for 70% of the red meat eaten globally.

Sadly, 40% of produce grown is never sold due to imperfections and "ugliness".

In 1961 Domino's Pizza cofounder James Monaghan traded his 50% stake to his brother Tom for a used VW Beetle a year after founding the pizza company. Tom sold his stake in the business 38 years later for $1 billion.

McDonald's originally sold hot dogs not burgers.

Ice cream company Ben & Jerry's was originally going to be a bagel company.

Lamborghini began by making farm equipment.

DID YOU KNOW?

The best-selling toy of all time is Rubik's Cube.

Starbucks uses over 93 million gallons of milk each year.

Nike's famous swoosh logo cost them $35 dollars and the design student who created it was gifted a diamond-encrusted ring in the shape of the emblem years later.

BP once paid out $211 million on a logo redesign.

Twitter's famous blue bird logo is named Larry.

Yahoo is an acronym: Yet Another Hierarchical Officious Oracle.

Jack Daniel's employees get a whiskey bottle every month on payday.

DID YOU KNOW?

Pulling the perfect pint of Guinness takes 119.5 seconds while pouring at an incline of 45 degrees.

Baskin Robbins once made ketchup-flavored ice cream.

Puma & Adidas were founded by brothers who once ran a shoe company together but went their separate ways.

Employees of Ben & Jerry's get to take home three free pints of ice cream every day.

If a Google employee dies, their spouse receives half their pay for 10 years as well as stock benefits and any children receive $1000 per month until they turn 19.

Rather than paying landscapers to mow their campus, Google has 200 goats to mow & fertilize the campus lawns.

DID YOU KNOW?

The Shell Oil Company began as a novelty shop in London that sold seashells.

Microsoft made $16,005 revenue in their first year of operation.

The Marlboro Man died of lung cancer.

Dell Computers was started by a 19-year-old with only $1000.

The Gmail logo was designed the night before it was launched.

Every year Louis Vuitton burns all unsold bags to prevent them from being sold at a lower price.

Google was originally called Backrub.

DID YOU KNOW?

The Facebook color scheme is blue because Mark Zuckerberg suffers from red-green color blindness.

The popular mobile game app Candy Crush brings in more than $633,000 in revenue every day.

Pepsi got it's name from pepsin, a digestive enzyme. The inventor of the drink believed it was a "healthy" cola that aided digestion.

The name Volkswagen means "peoples car" in German.

The CIA reads 5 million tweets daily.

The original name of Amazon was "Cadabra" but was changed after Bezos' lawyer misheard it as "Cadaver".

DID YOU KNOW?

The name Adobe came from the river Adobe Creek that ran behind the house of Adobe Systems Inc's cofounder John Warnock.

Burj Khalifa is the tallest building in the world.

Levi Strauss was an aristocrat and didn't wear his brand of denim because they were meant for the working class.

Bill Gates is estimated to make between $8-11 million per day.

Elon Musk is estimated to make more than $54 million per day.

Colonel Sanders (KFC founder) had his secret recipe rejected over 1000 times before a restaurant finally added it to the menu.

DID YOU KNOW?

Cereal brands are the second largest advertiser on television today, behind automobiles.

Samsung accounts for 20% of Korea's GDP.

Burt's Bees is owned by Clorox.

Studies have shown the most productive day of the workweek is Tuesday.

Changing the U.S. $1 bill to a $1 coin would save the U.S. $4.4 billion over 30 years.

More people worldwide have mobile phones than toilets.

Starbucks spends more on employee health insurance ($300 million) than on coffee beans.

Apple had a 3rd founder, Ronald Wayne, who had a 10% stake in the company but chose to forfeit his shares 12 days into the fledgling company for $800, which would be worth almost $100 billion today.

Robert Chesebrough, inventor of Vaseline, ate a spoonful of it every morning.

70% of small businesses in the U.S. are owned & operated by a single person.

In iPhone ads the time is always 9:42 a.m. or 9:41 a.m. because Apple events start at 9 a.m. and big product reveals generally happen 40 minutes into the presentation.

One in eight American workers have been employed by McDonald's.

The world's 100 richest people earned enough in 2012 to end global poverty four times over.

DID YOU KNOW?

More than 80 million "mouse ears" have been sold at Walt Disney World.

Gambling generates more revenue than movies, spectator sports, theme parks, cruise ships and recorded music combined.

In response to the air pollution in China, millionaire Chen Guangbiao began selling fresh air in a can, selling eight million cans in 10 days and earning $6 million in a year.

The world's largest package delivery company, UPS, was founded by two teens with a bicycle and $100 borrowed from a friend.

In 1999, Google's founders were willing to sell the company to a web portal called Excite for under $1 million, but Excite passed on the offer.

DID YOU KNOW?

In 1974, FedEx was on the verge of bankruptcy but was saved when the founder took the last $5000 of the company's assets and turned it into $32,000 gambling in Las Vegas. In 2018, FedEx generated over $65 billion.

In 1971 Astronaut Alan Shepherd smuggled a golf club and ball onto the moon and played golf.

MLB umpires always wear black underwear in case their trousers split.

There are over 8000 sports played worldwide, but only 33 sports were played at the 2021 Olympic Games.

Babe Ruth wore a cabbage leaf under his cap for good luck & to help him stay cool.

DID YOU KNOW?

NBA superstar Michael Jordan didn't make his high school basketball team as a sophomore, but continued to practice and made the team the next year.

If Wayne Gretzky had never scored a single goal, he would still be the NHL's all-time points leader based on his assists alone.

There are only 18 minutes of action in the average 2.5 hour MLB game.

The Stanley Cup's real name is the Dominion Hockey Challenge Cup.

Winners in the Olympics were not originally awarded gold medals, instead they were given a silver medal and an olive branch.

The silhouette on the official NBA logo is L.A. Lakers guard Jerry West.

DID YOU KNOW?

The world record for the most nonstop pushups is 10,507 by Minoru Yoshida of Japan.

NFL referees also receive Super Bowl rings, though they are smaller and less impressive than player rings.

When volleyball first began it was played with a basketball bladder.

Until 1936 the basketball jump ball took place at center court after every single made basket.

Badminton was initially called "Poona".

There are exactly 108 stitches on a baseball.

Mouthguards are optional in both the NFL & NHL.

DID YOU KNOW?

In the original basketball rules dribbling was not allowed, you had to toss the ball to another player to keep the game going.

Before an NHL game, hockey pucks are frozen to make them glide smoother and reduce bouncing.

North Dakota has the most golf courses per capita of any U.S. state.

During the 1943 season due to losing many players to WWII military service, the Pittsburgh Steeler & Philadelphia Eagles combined teams to become the Steagles.

The blades in figure skates were originally made from animal bones.

During a tennis match, a player runs 3 miles.

DID YOU KNOW?

The Oreo cookie-to-creme ratio is always 71% cookie to 29% creme.

Ramen noodles were invented to fulfill demand for soup during WWII food shortages in Japan.

Starburst candies were originally called Opal Fruits.

A janitor invented Flamin' Hot Cheetos by sprinkling chili powder on original cheetos. He presented the idea to execs and is now an executive VP at PepsiCo's North American division.

Soldiers in the Spanish Civil War who ate pieces of chocolate covered in sugar coating inspired Forrest Mars to manufacture M&M's with a shell to prevent melting.

DID YOU KNOW?

NC State University holds an annual Krispy Kreme challenge which is a race that requires you to run 5 miles and consume 12 donuts within an hour.

The Frito-Lay plant in Georgia cooks almost 1 million pounds of potatoes every day to make an average of 175,000 boxes of Lay's. They buy around 4 billion pounds of potatoes each year from 165 farms across the country.

Hershey's facility in Hershey, PA makes 70 million foil-wrapped Kisses every day.

Planters Peanuts have been sold since 1890 but the Mr. Peanut mascot began in 1916 when a 14 year old submitted a sketch for a trademark contest and he was paid $5 for his winning design.

DID YOU KNOW?

Reese's Pieces goal is 50% orange, 25% brown and 25% yellow in each box.

To better fit in with the city's natural southwestern colors, the McDonald's in Sedona, Arizona has turquoise arches instead of it's traditional yellow.

Oscar Mayer debuted it's popular Wienermobile in 1936, a 13 foot long vehicle shaped like a giant hog dog on wheels.

Cocoa Puffs debuted it's mascot in 1962, Sonny the Cuckoo Bird.

Popular restaurant chain Texas Roadhouse is actually headquartered in Louisville, Kentucky, not in Texas.

The first woman athlete to appear on a Wheaties box was golfer Babe Didrikson in 1935.

DID YOU KNOW?

Mondelez Intl, formerly known as Kraft Foods, got it's name from combining the latin words for "world" and "delicious". It is based in Chicago and owns Cadbury, Chips Ahoy and Oreo, among others.

Ore-Ida got it's name from an abbreviation for the two states in which some of their original potato fields were located: Oregon & Idaho.

Maxwell House was started in 1892 by a grocer and was named after a hotel in Nashville, TN which was the brand's largest customer. It was the highest-selling coffee in the U.S. for almost 100 years.

Actor Paul Newman's charitable Newman's Own Foundation has donated over $600 million to charity since 1982.

DID YOU KNOW?

Actors and celebrities are famous for their stage names. Here are some of their real birth names:

Katy Perry = Kathryn Hudson
Bruno Mars = Peter Gene Hernandez
Lady Gaga = Stefani Germanotta
Rihanna = Robyn Fenty
Lana Del Rey = Elizabeth Grant
Miley Cyrus = Destiny Hope Cyrus
Jamie Foxx = Eric Marlon Bishop
Blake Lively = Blake Ellender Brown
Drake = Aubrey Graham
Natalie Portman = Neta-Lee Hershlag
Frank Ocean = Christopher Edwin Breaux
Cardi B = Belcalis Almanzar
Eminem = Marshall Mathers
Whoopi Goldberg = Caryn Johnson
Ben Kingsley = Krishna Bhanji
Bea Arthur = Bernice Frankel
Vin Diesel = Mark Vincent
Helen Mirren = Ilyena Mironov
Snoop Dogg = Calvin Broadus Jr.

DID YOU KNOW?

Speaking of celebrities, there are some interesting connections between some:

- Jeff Bezos is a distant cousin to country singer George Strait
- President Obama counts President George Bush as his 10th cousin and Brad Pitt as a 9th cousin
- Cameron Diaz is Nicole Richie's sister-in-law
- Melissa & Jenny McCarthy are first cousins
- Brandy is cousins with Snoop Dog
- Diana Ross is Ashlee Simpson's mother-in-law
- Emily Blunt is Stanley Tucci's sister-in-law
- Dionne Warwick is Whitney Houston's cousin
- Mariska Hargitay's mother was late actor Jayne Mansfield
- Sofia Coppola & Nicholas Cage are cousins

DID YOU KNOW?

Alaska is the largest U.S. state by area.

California has the most national parks.

Rhode Island is the smallest U.S. state by area.

Alaska has the longest coastline of any U.S. state.

Wyoming is the U.S. state with the lowest population density.

The Great Basin Desert is the largest desert in the U.S.

Missouri River is the longest river in the U.S.

Yosemite Falls, California is the tallest waterfall in the U.S.

Long Beach, Washington is the longest beach in the U.S.

DID YOU KNOW?

The first pizza made in the U.S. was in New York City.

The first cheeseburger was served in Colorado.

The first ice cream sundae was made in Wisconsin.

The largest porch swing in the world is located in Hebron, Nebraska and it can sit 25 adults.

Boeing's primary manufacturing site in Everett, Washington completed in 1966 has 4.2 million square feet of floor area and spans 100 acres. It produces four aircraft types and has 2.33 miles of pedestrian tunnels beneath the manufacturing floor.

DID YOU KNOW?

The second largest football stadium in the world is Michigan Stadium in Ann Arbor, MI with a capacity of 107,601.

Stratolaunch constructed a 500,000 pound jet designed to travel at 35,000 feet. It's wingspan measures 385 feet in width and will launch rockets that will then use their own motors to push themselves into space. It has 6 engines and 28 wheels and will be used to transfer rockets carrying satellites into the Earth's upper atmosphere.

General Sherman is the world's tallest tree reaching 275 feet tall and more than 36 feet wide. It is located in Three Rivers, CA.

New South China Mall is the world's largest mall and can house 2350 stores in it's 6.46 million square feet. It is located in Dongguan, China.

DID YOU KNOW?

The world's largest swimming pool is located in a private resort in Algarroba, Chile and measures 3323 feet long, holds 250 million liters of water and spans 20 acres. The water source is the Pacific Ocean and the water is cleaned and filtered before use in the pool.

Robert Wadlow (1918-1940) from the U.S. was the tallest man in recorded history with a height of 8 ft 11 inches.

Irvin Gordon won a world record in 2014 for having the highest vehicle mileage on his 1966 Volvo 1800S which driving in Alaska. By May of 2014 he had driven just over 3 million miles in the vehicle.

Jeanne Louise Calment (France) was the oldest authenticated human living 122 years and 164 days. She died at a nursing home in France in August 1997.

DID YOU KNOW?

The white truffle is the world's most expensive fungus, costing up to $3000 per kilo. They can only be harvested with the help of trained dogs since they grow mostly underground.

The most expensive man-made object is the International Space Station (ISS). Final cost will be over $100 billion.

The longest monster truck is operated by Russ Mann (USA) and measures 32 ft long as of 2014. It was built to serve as a limo for Las Vegas tourists.

The longest bicycle is 180 ft 11 in and made in the Netherlands.

In 2016, Mozart sold more albums than Beyonce.

DID YOU KNOW?

2000 silkworm cocoons are needed to produce one pound of silk.

Ants can carry and lift more than 50x their own weight.

100 Monarch butterflies put together only weigh an ounce.

Women couldn't apply for credit at a bank until 1974.

Before the invention of modern false teeth, dentures were commonly made from the teeth of dead soldiers.

George Washington owned a whiskey distillery.

Theodore Roosevelt's kids had a pet bear, badger and hyena and they brought them all to the White House.

DID YOU KNOW?

You're never farther than 30 steps from a trash can at Disney World.

90% of Libya is desert.

Pilots and co-pilots are required to eat different meals before flights so they don't both end up with food poisoning.

The Great Barrier Reef is so large it can be seen from outer space.

The ice in Antarctica is made up of almost 3% penguin urine.

President Nixon was an accomplished musician who played five instruments, including the accordian.

None of The Beatles could read music.

DID YOU KNOW?

Oreo has constructed an asteroid proof bunker in Norway to store their recipes and cookies in case of an apocalypse.

The name "Canada" comes from a Native American word that means "Big Village" or "Settlement".

The oldest unopened 1.5 liter bottle of wine was found in a Roman tomb that is nearly 1700 years old.

An arctic fox changes it's fur color to match the season. In winter it is white and in summer it is brown.

In Dubai, supercars like Ferrari & Lamborghini are used by McDonald's for deliveries.

The sound an ATM produces is not the rollers delivering the cash. It is produced by a speaker to reassure you money is on the way.

DID YOU KNOW?

The Guinness Book of World Records was invented by the Guinness Brewery as they figured a verifiable fact book would halt bar arguments.

Millions of trees in the world are started by squirrels who bury nuts then forget where they buried them.

The human nose can detect 1 trillion different scents.

Bananas grow upside down.

Butterflies taste with their feet.

The world's oldest astronomical clock is in operation in Prague, installed in 1410.

Diphylleia grayi is called the "skeleton flower" because it turns transparent when it rains then reverts to white when dry.

DID YOU KNOW?

Cockroach milk is 4x as nutritious as cow's milk.

The hottest chili pepper in the world is called the Dragon's Breath chili pepper and is so hot it could kill you.

Rolls Royce uses the leather of 15-18 bulls per car, raised only in cold climates to prevent marks from insect bites.

There is a heart shaped island in Croatia known as "Island of Love".

Volkswagon owns Bentley, Bugatti, Lamborghini, Audi, Ducati and Porsche.

France is the most visited country in the world boasting over 89 million annual visitors.

Iceland has the cleanest air in the world.

DID YOU KNOW?

It cost $7.5 million to build the Titanic ship and $200 million to make the *Titanic* movie.

In Morocco goats climb trees and graze there in herds, eating the fruits of the Argan tree (from which nuts are made into fragrant oil.)

In Norway every citizen's income is made publicly available for anyone to review.

The world's deepest and oldest freshwater lake is Lake Baikal in Russia. It reaches a maximum depth of 5387 feet and contains 20% of the world's unfrozen fresh water.

Bees live less than 40 days, visit at least 1000 flowers and produce less than a teaspoon of honey in their lifetimes.

There are enough restaurants in New York City for one person to eat out every night for 54 years and never eat twice at the same place.

DID YOU KNOW?

The average Japanese train delay is just 18 seconds, they are considered the world's most punctual trains.

The bagworm moth caterpillar collects and saws tiny sticks to construct elaborate log cabins to live in.

A leech has 10 stomachs, 32 brains, 9 pair of testicles & several hundred teeth.

For most people, the length of your forearm is roughly the same length as your foot.

During summertime heat, the Eiffel Tower can be up to 6 inches taller as the iron heats up due to thermal expansion.

Quokkas are considered the happiest animals in the world.

DID YOU KNOW?

Snail teeth are the strongest biological material on Earth and can withstand pressure high enough to turn carbon into diamond.

Niagara Falls froze completely solid during the winter of 1848 for 30 hours.

Amazon's largest warehouse is the size of 17 American football fields.

It would take 12 million mosquitoes sucking at once to completely drain a human of blood.

Iceland has no army and has consistently been ranked as the most peaceful country in the world.

Macchu Picchu, Peru, attracts over 1.5 million visitors each year.

DID YOU KNOW?

Komodo dragons are the largest living lizard, typically weighing around 154 pounds. The largest verified one weighed 366 pounds and measured 10.3 feet long.

The Wulingyuan Scenic Area in Hunan Province, China, features over 3000 quartzite sandstone pillars and served as the inspiration for the floating mountains in *Avatar* movie.

The ring colors on the Olympic flag stand for regions: blue represents Oceania, green represents Europe; black represents Africa; red represents America and yellow represents Asia.

The Devil's Bridge in Kromlau, Germany was designed to make a perfect circle with it's reflection in the water below.

The first known billionaire was John D. Rockefeller from New York.

DID YOU KNOW?

The longest recorded time without sleep is 453 hours and 40 minutes by Robert McDonald in 1986 which set a Guiness World Record. They no longer monitor the record due to the inherent dangers associated with sleep deprivation.

———·———

There are a bunch of categories the Guiness Book of World Records no longer monitors for various reasons, including:

———·———

Mass Balloon Release (due to safety of animals and plane interference)

Longest Survival Without Food
Longest Survival Without Water
Largest Meal Eaten
(all for health & safety concerns)

Most Beer Drunk In An Hour
(due to health & safety concerns)

DID YOU KNOW?

Longest Kiss
(due to sleep deprivation concerns)

Largest Car Tire Burnout Image
(due to environmental concerns)

Fastest Yodel
(it was deemed too subjective)

Fastest Violin Player
(impossible to tell if all notes correct)

Heaviest Living Cat
(due to health & safety concerns)

Most Spiders On The Body For 30 Sec
(due to animal welfare concerns)

Largest Audience At Camel Wrestling Festival
(due to animal welfare concerns)

DID YOU KNOW?

Bill Hast injected himself with snake venom for a few years to build up an immunity. He survived 172 snakebites, donated his blood to snakebite victims & lived 100 years.

Bear Grylls holds the world record for the highest open air formal dinner party held in a hot air balloon at 7600 meters.

The head of a dead snake can still bite and inject venom for hours after it's death due to lingering reflexes.

The oldest living land animal on earth is a 192 year old tortoise named Jonathan.

The hardest bone in the human body is the femur.

A group of owls is called a parliament.

A silverback gorilla can lift over 1763 pounds.

DID YOU KNOW?

Giraffes are 30 times more likely to get hit by lightning then people.

Identical twins don't have the same fingerprints.

Earth's rotation is slowing which increases the length of a day by 1.8 seconds per century.

The deepest part of the ocean is 35,876 feet down.

Caesar salad was invented in 1924 by Caesar Cardini at his restaurant in Tijuana, Mexico.

The sun is around 400 times larger than the moon.

The average person blinks 14-17 times per minute.

DID YOU KNOW?

90% of the world's population lives in the Northern Hemisphere.

Honey never spoils.

A chicken in the 1940s once lived for 18 months without a head. Mike the chicken survived because his jugular vein and most of his brainstem were left mostly intact, ensuring just enough brain function for survival.

Central Park in NYC is larger than the country of Monaco.

The average golf ball has 336 dimples.

Wearing a tie can reduce bloodflow to the brain by 7.5%.

Over 60% of the world's lakes are located in Canada.

DID YOU KNOW?

The International Space Station orbits Earth approx every 90 minutes.

The fear of long words is called Hippopotomonstrosesquippedaliophobia.

The world's oldest cat lived to 38 years and 3 days old and was named Creme Puff.

Cuvier's beaked whales can hold their breath underwater for over two hours.

Between 50-80% of earth's living organisms are in the ocean.

Mount Everest isn't the tallest mountain on Earth, Mauna Kea & Mauna Loa in Hawaii (the twin volcanoes) are taller due to 4.2km of their height being submerged underwater.

The world's oldest dog lived to 29.5 years old and was named Bluey.

DID YOU KNOW?

Octopuses don't have tentacles. Scientists define tentacles as limbs with suckers at the end. Octopus arms have suckers down most of their length.

———·———

Australia is wider than the moon.

———·———

Allodoxaphobia is the fear of other people's opinions.

———·———

Venus is the only planet to spin clockwise.

———·———

Ants don't have lungs. They breathe through spiracles, nine or ten tiny openings.

———·———

Statistically, football teams wearing red play better and win more home matches than any other color.

———·———

Snails have between 1,000 - 12,000 tiny teeth all over it's filelike tongue

DID YOU KNOW?

Signatures can reveal personality traits. In a 2016 study, men with a larger signature correlated with higher social bravado and women with a larger signature correlated with narcissistic traits.

Finland is the happiest country on Earth for six years in a row.

Hippos can't swim, instead they perform a slow-motion gallop on the riverbed or sea floor. They can also sleep underwater thanks to a built-in reflex allowing them to bob up, take a breath and sink back down without waking up.

Human teeth are the only part of the body that cannot heal themselves.

Lemons float in water but limes sink.

The Eiffel Tower was originally made for Barcelona, not Paris.